Introduction

Enjoy traditional folding fun! "Origami" is a very old paper-folding technique that originated in Asia. For a long time, it was an integral part of religious ceremonies, and in Japan, the folded crane is still considered a symbol of good luck. The kawaii-style designs will give a playful, fun look to your origami and with this book, you can quickly and easily fold beautiful shapes.

On the following pages, you will find a selection of varied folding instructions that will help you create impressive creations. In addition to the illustrated step-by-step instructions, there are also short videos for most designs that can be accessed on digital devices via the QR code below. This makes folding the projects even easier! With the 333 colorful papers, there are endless combinations and folding possibilities.

Happy folding!

The Basics

BASIC SHAPE: KITE

1. To make a diagonal fold, position the paper so that one corner is facing you. Take the corner and fold it over to meet the opposite corner. Make a crease and then unfold the sheet.

2. Fold the outer edges of the paper inward to line up with the diagonal crease you have just made.

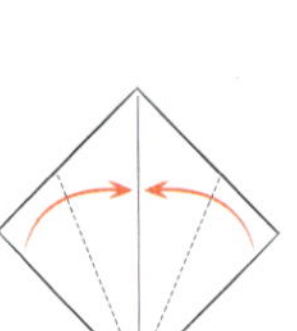

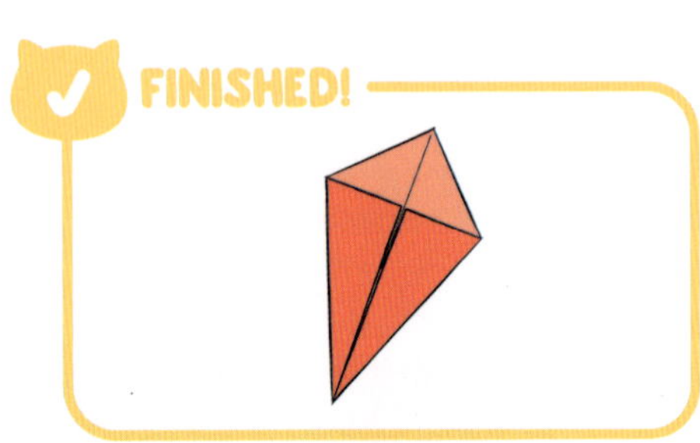

ZIGZAG FOLD

1. Fold the paper inward along the first marked line and outward along the second.

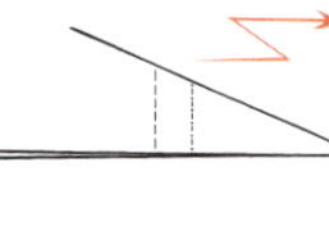

2. Now fold inward again along the second fold and outward again along the first fold.

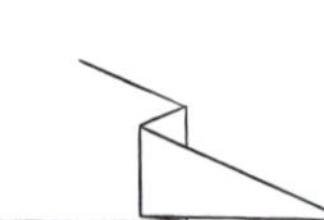

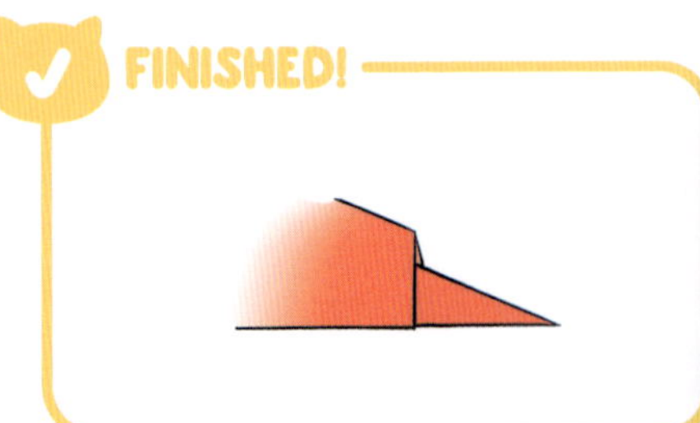

INSIDE REVERSE FOLD

1. Fold the tip inward and then unfold.

2. Gently pull the sides outward and fold the point down (between the sides).

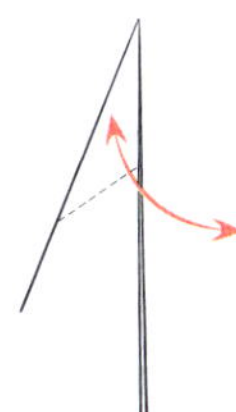

OUTSIDE REVERSE FOLD

1. Fold the tip inward and then unfold.

2. Gently pull the sides outward and down, and fold the point over them (over the sides).

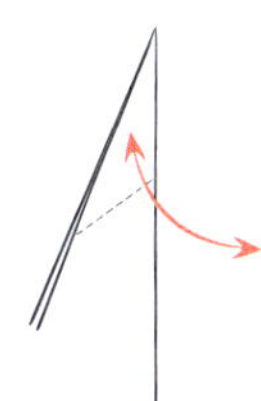

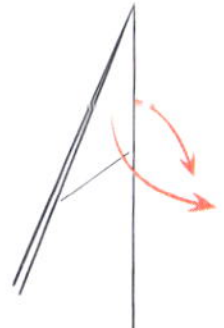

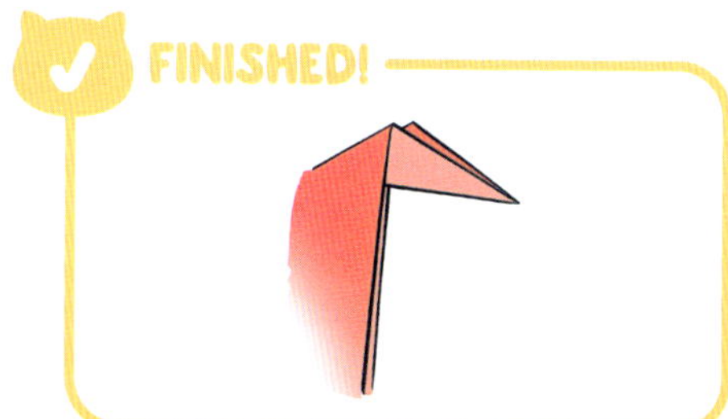

Cat

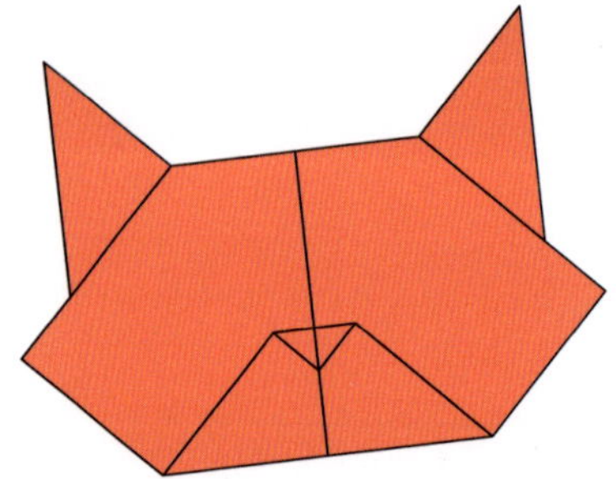

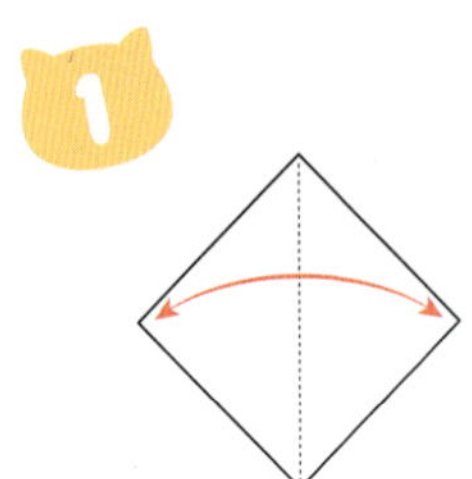

Fold the left corner over to the right corner and back again.

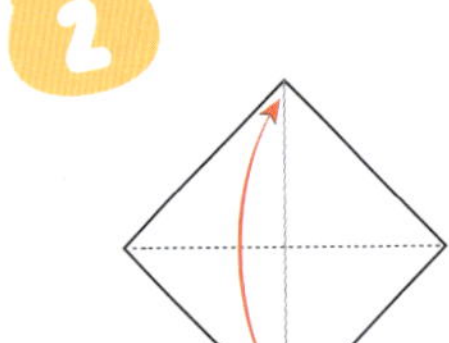

Fold the bottom corner over the top corner and back again.

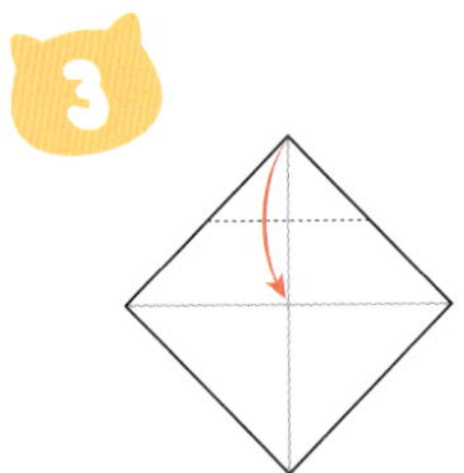

Now fold the top corner to the center of the sheet.

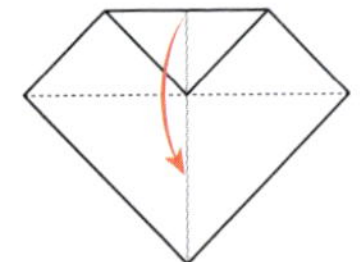

Fold the top edge down along the center line made in Step 2.

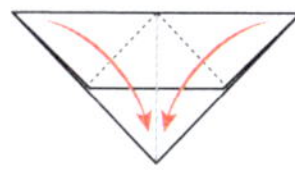

Fold the left and right tips to the bottom corner.

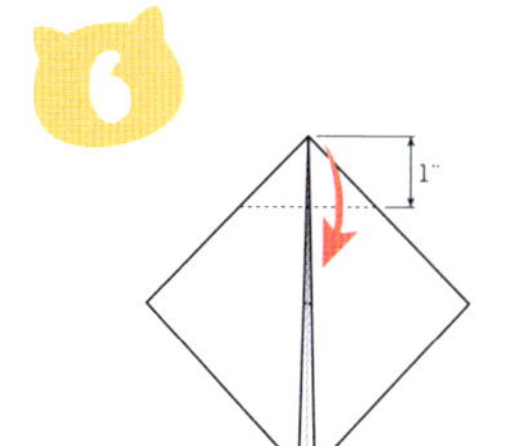

Fold the top corner down.

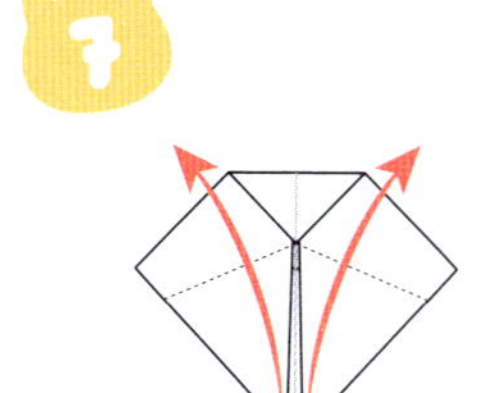

Fold the two bottom points (without the backing behind them) upwards.

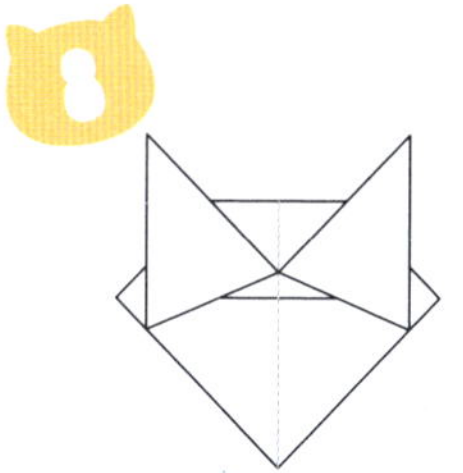

Then smooth out the folds, turn the model over...

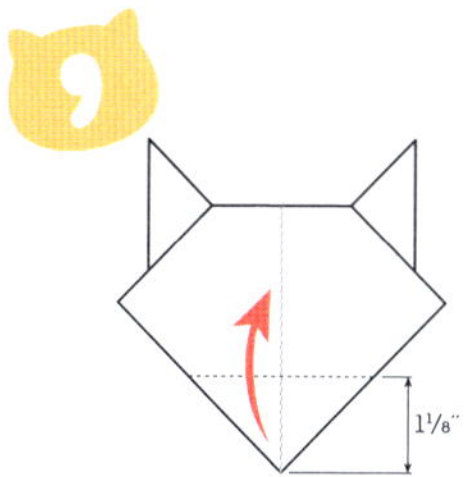

... and fold the bottom corner upwards.

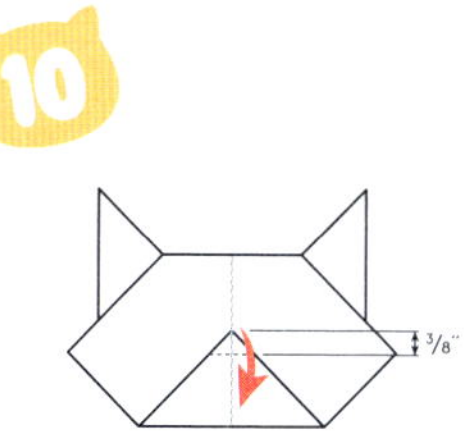

Fold the tip of your nose down slightly.

Butterfly

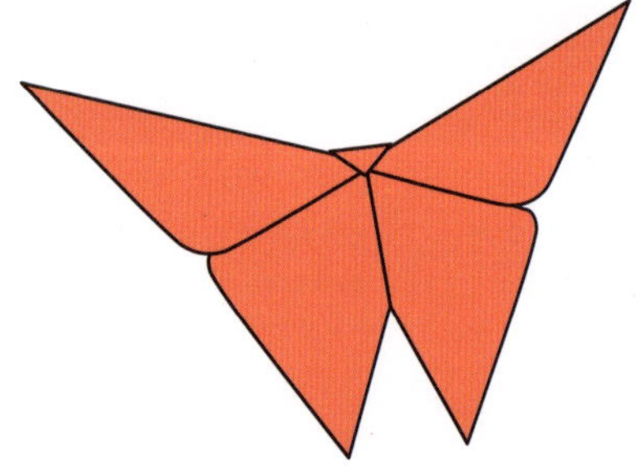

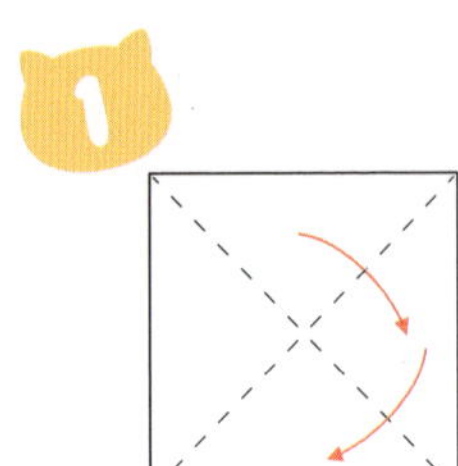

Fold the two diagonals. Unfold the sheet completely again.

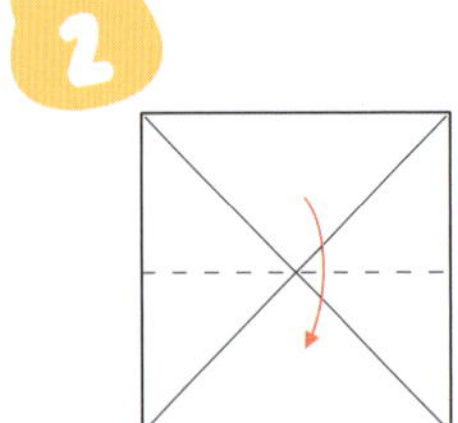

Now fold the top edge over the bottom edge.

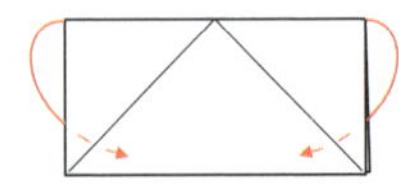

Push the corners toward each other to form a triangle. The corners will virtually disappear inside the triangle.

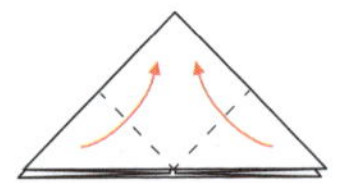

Fold the top layer of the right and left corners to the triangle point.

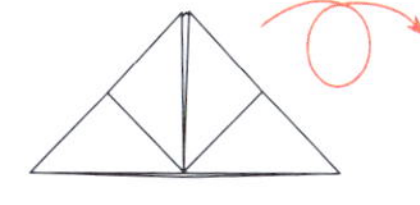

Rotate 180° and flip over.

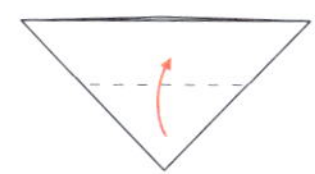

If you extend the tip of the triangle slightly beyond the top edge, the lower wings will bend upward slightly and become tense.

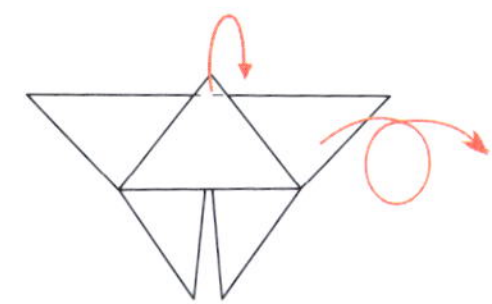

Fold the small tip to the other side and turn the folded piece over.

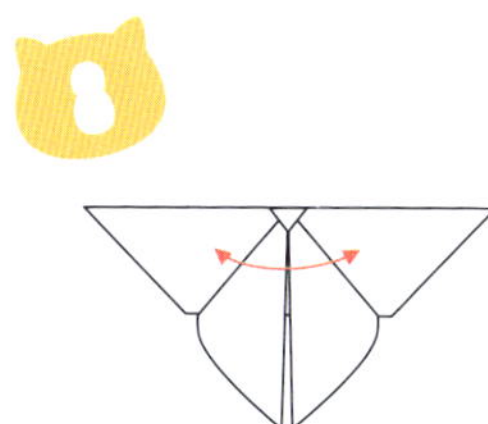

Fold the wings upwards in the middle toward you.

Fox

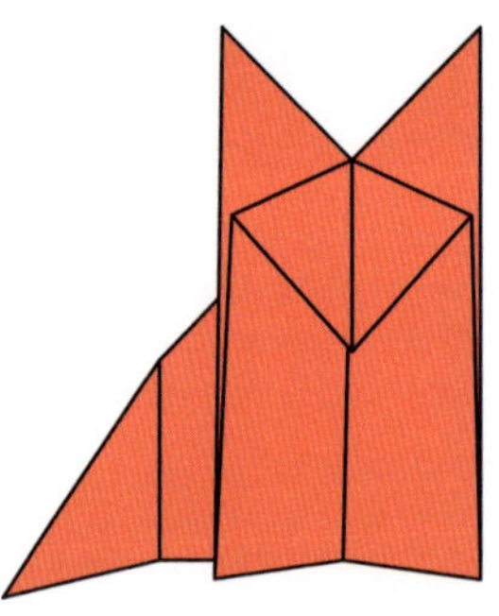

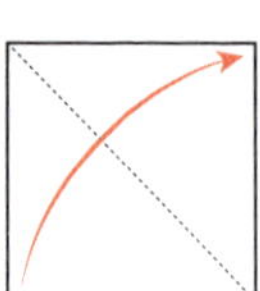

Fold the bottom left corner diagonally to the top right corner.

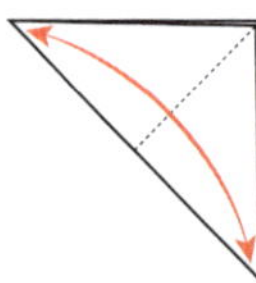

Now fold the lower right point over the upper left point and back again.

3

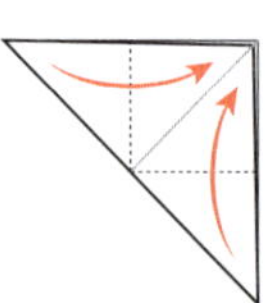

Fold the same two points to the top right corner.

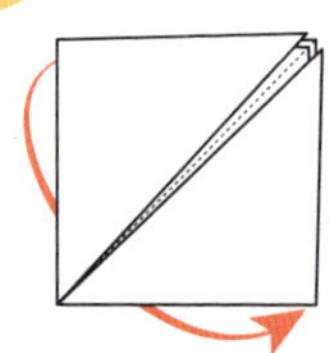

Fold the top left corner backward to the bottom right corner.

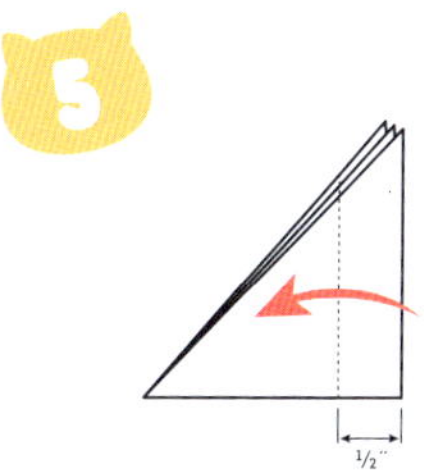

Fold the right edges of all three layers of paper to the left.

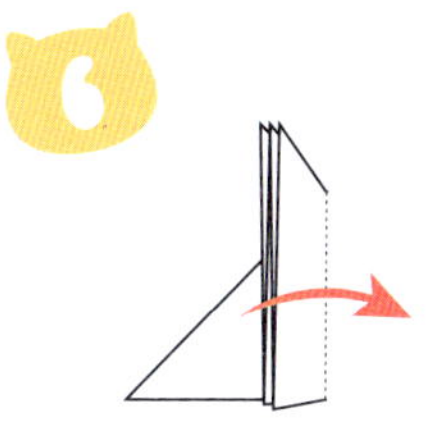

Then fold the top layer of paper back to the right so that the three layers spread out.

To fold the fox head, simply press the middle layer down.

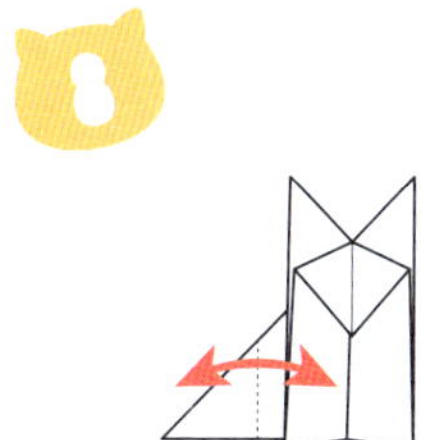

Finally, fold the left tip to the right to the center of the front feet and back again. This is the foxtail.

Rabbit

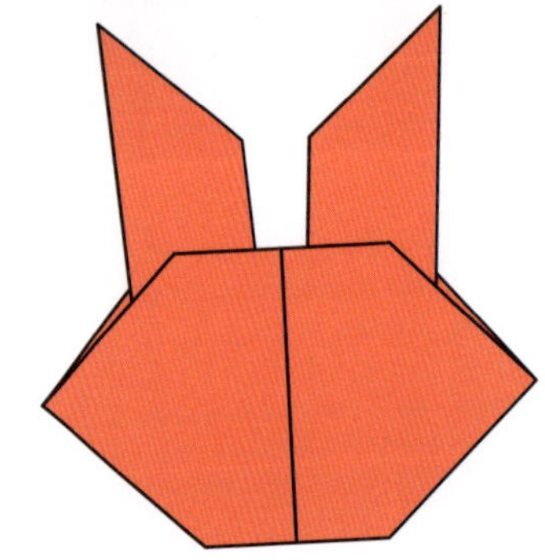

1

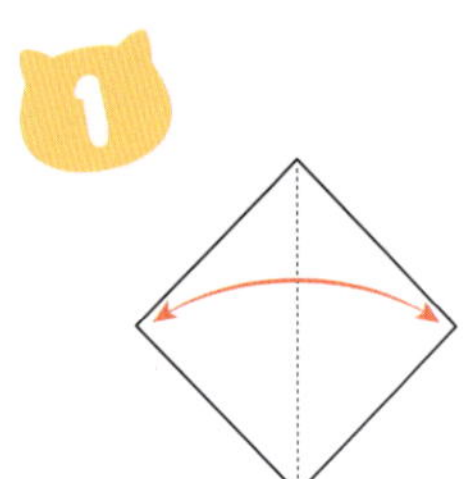

Fold the paper in half (left corner to right corner) and then unfold it again.

2

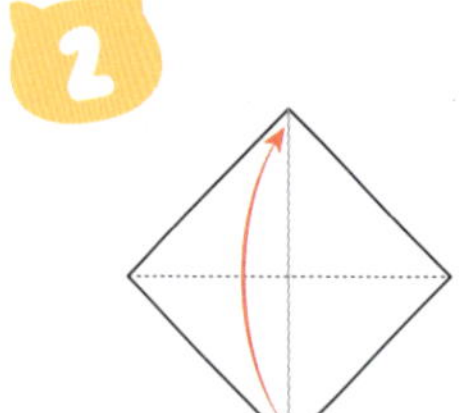

Now fold the bottom corner over the top corner.

3

Fold the bottom edge upwards.

4

Fold the two top corners down as shown.

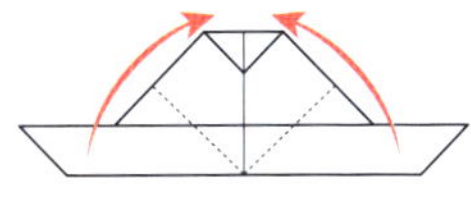

Fold the right and left bottom edges upwards almost to the center line.

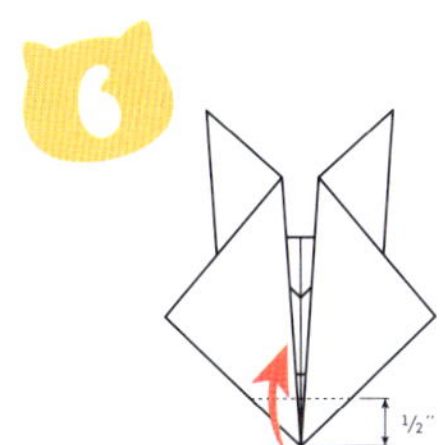

Finally, fold the bottom corner upwards.

Smooth out the folds and turn the model over.

Heart

1

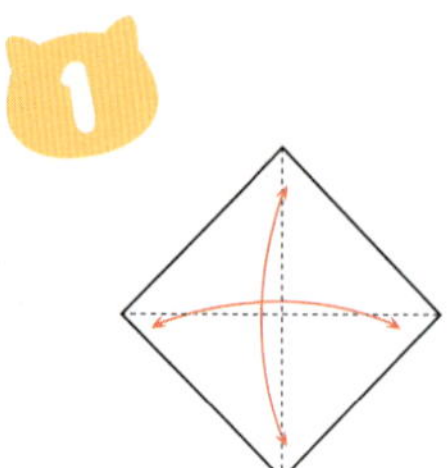

Fold two diagonals by placing each opposite corner together, creasing the paper and opening each fold.

2

Fold the top corner toward the center.

3

Fold the bottom corner towards the top edge.

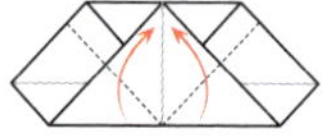

Fold the bottom left and right edges to the middle and turn the whole thing over.

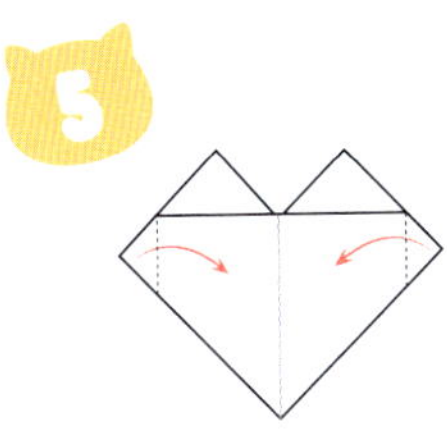

Fold the left and right corners towards the center.

Fold the top two corners down.

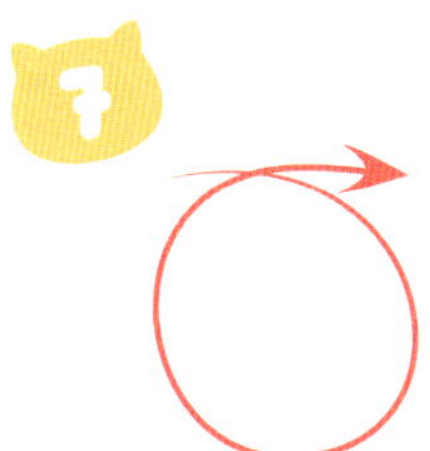

Turn the whole thing over.

Fish

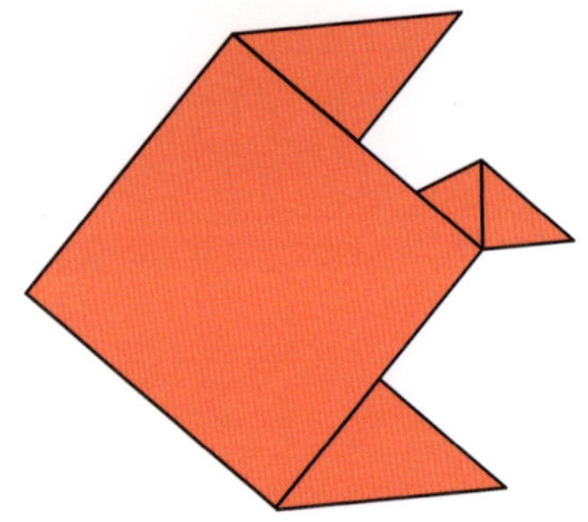

1

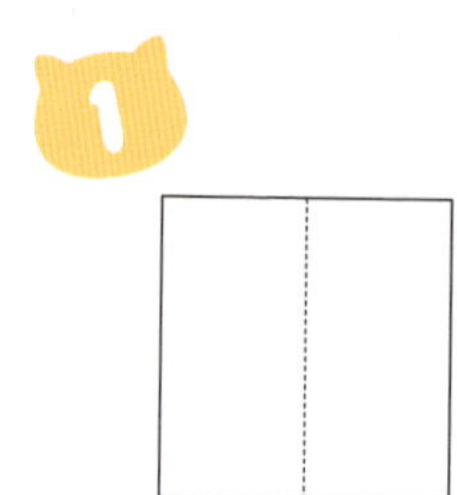

Place the sheet with the pattern facing down and fold along the center line. Open the paper.

2

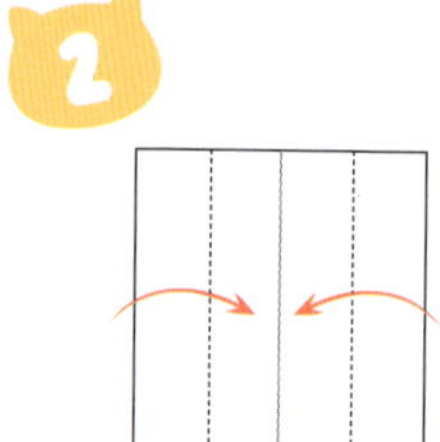

Place the folded piece with one edge toward you. Fold the right and left edges to the center line.

3

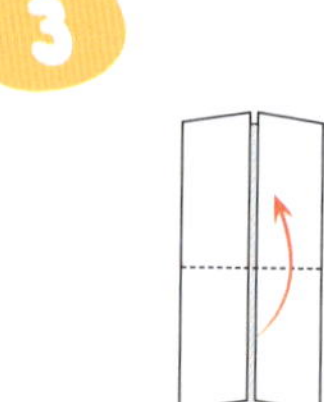

Fold the bottom edge to the top edge and open the fold again.

4

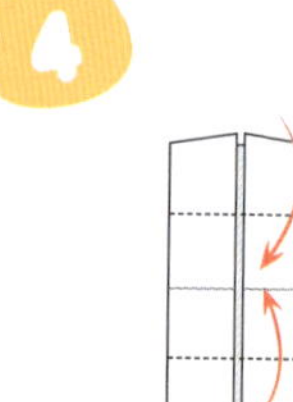

Fold the bottom and top edges toward the center.

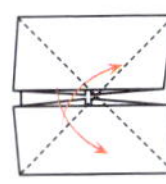

Fold two diagonals through the newly created, reduced square.

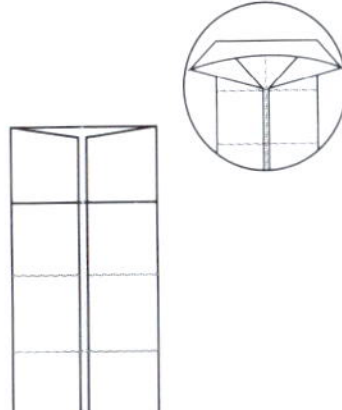

Fold one side of the square upwards and fold the top paper to the sides, creating two triangles.

7

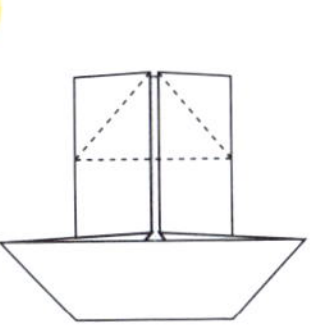

Turn the folding unit 180°, fold the other edge upwards and proceed as described in Step 6.

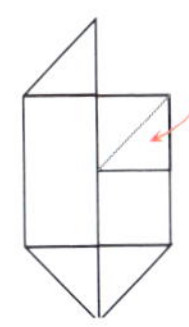

Turn the folded piece 90°. Open the upper right triangle and fold it into a small square towards the center.

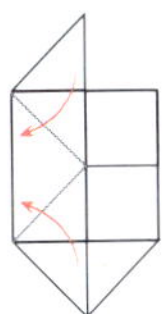

Fold the two left triangles to the left along the fold line.

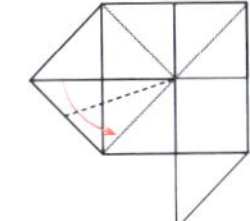

For the fin, fold the lower of the two triangles down and turn the whole thing over.

Pinwheel

1

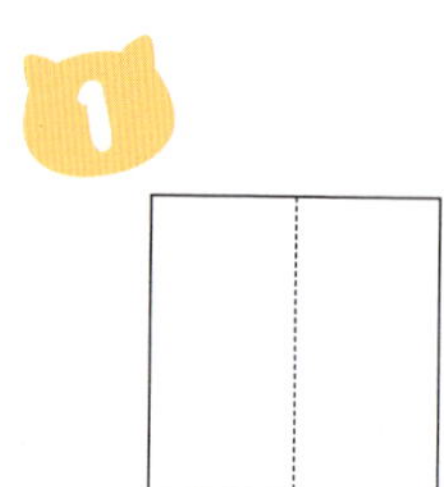

Place the sheet pattern-side down and fold along a center line. Open the paper.

2

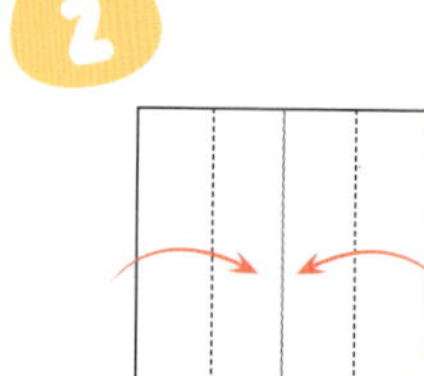

Place the folded piece with one edge toward you. Fold the right and left edges to the center line.

3

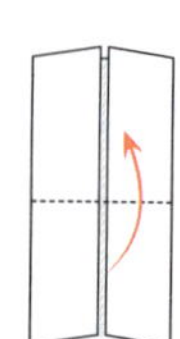

Fold the bottom edge to the top edge and open the fold again.

4

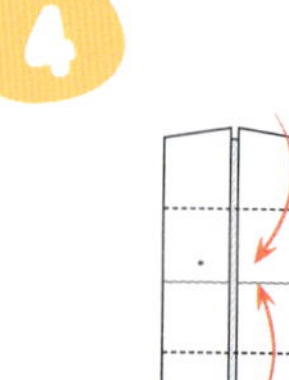

Fold the bottom and top edges toward the center.

Fold two diagonals through the newly created, reduced square.

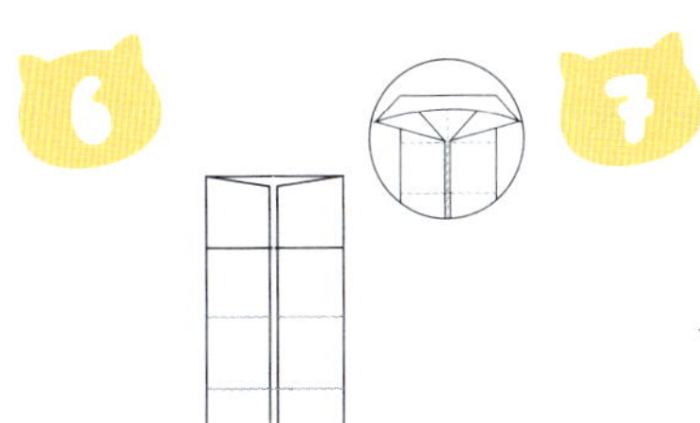

Fold one side of the square upwards and fold the top paper to the sides, creating two triangles.

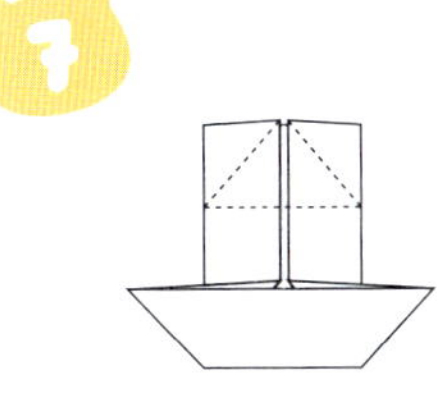

Turn the folded unit 180°, fold the other edge upward and proceed as in Step 6.

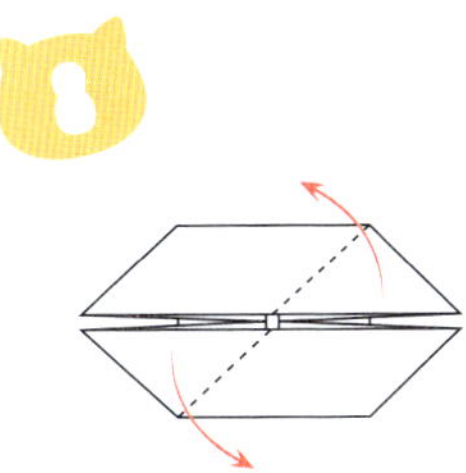

Fold the right corner up and the left corner down.

Lily

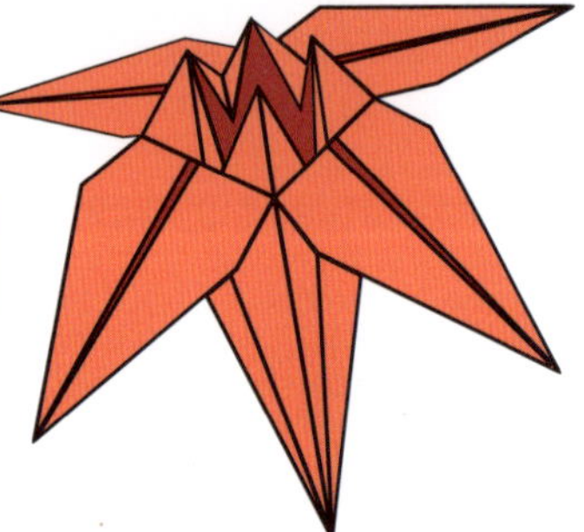

The Lily is a challenging shape to fold. Don't forget there is a video to follow! See page 1.

1

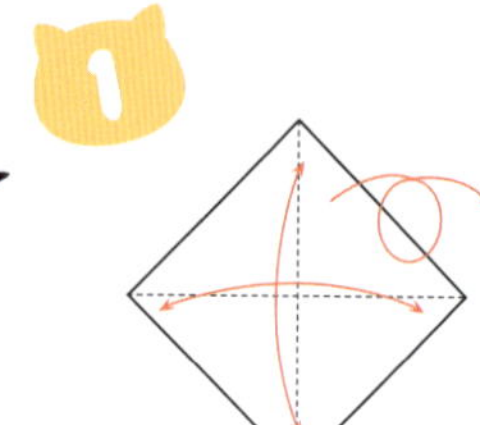

Fold the two diagonals, open the sheet, and turn it over.

2

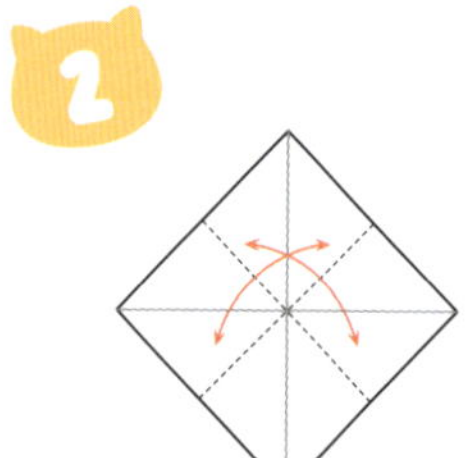

Now fold the two parallel diagonals and open the sheet again.

3

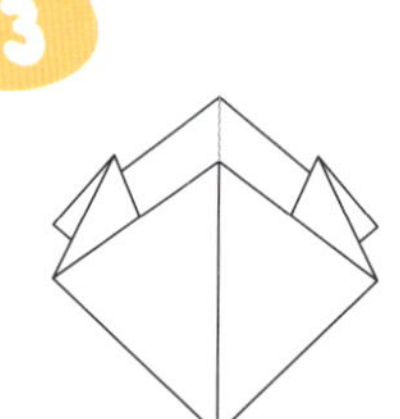

Move the two side fold lines to the center and fold the sheet into a square.

4

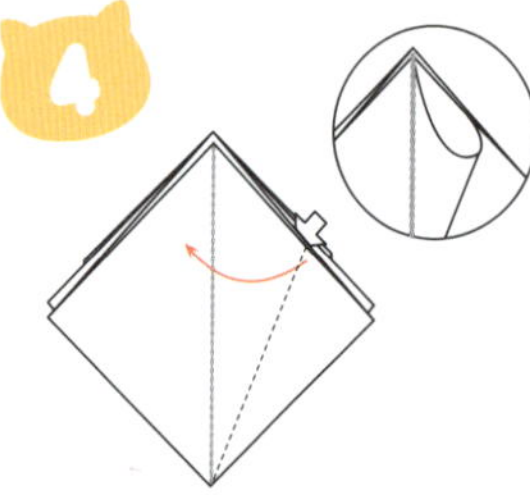

Take the top layer of the sheet and fold the right edge toward the center. Open it out and fold the corner from the inside out over the center of the square.

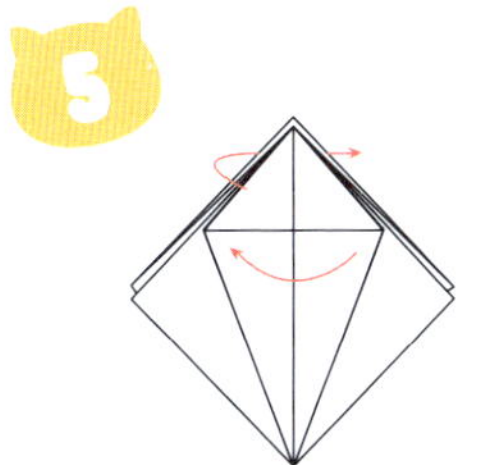

Fold the right corner to the left and repeat Step 4 until you get the shape shown in the next step.

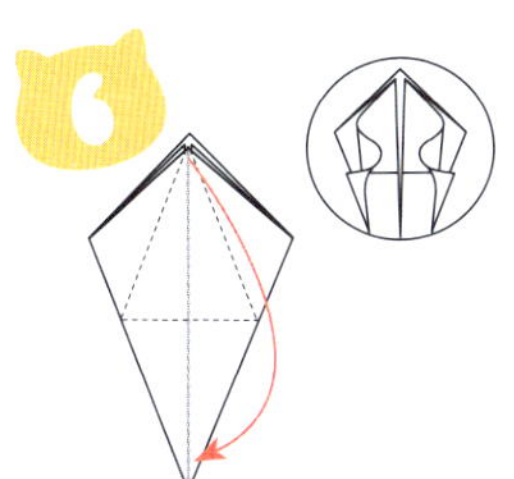

Create the triangle shown using crease lines. Now fold the top layer down. Fold the right side over the left side and repeat this process.

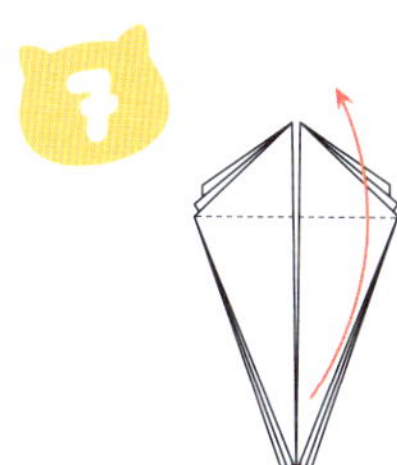

Fold the tip of the top layer upward.

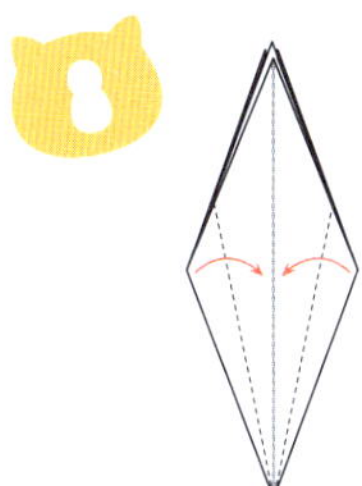

Fold the left and right corners to the center and repeat this step in turn.

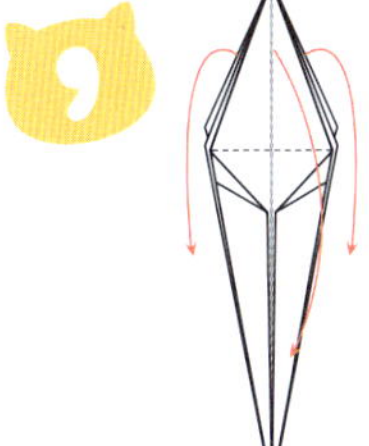

Fold the tips down to form petals and use a pencil to shape them into an outward curve.

Crane

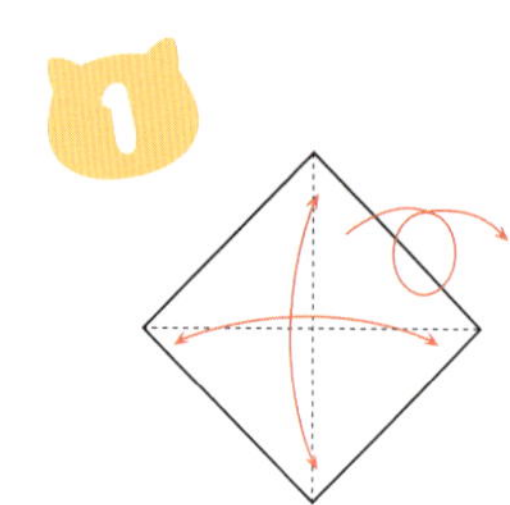

1

Fold the two diagonals, open the sheet, and turn it over.

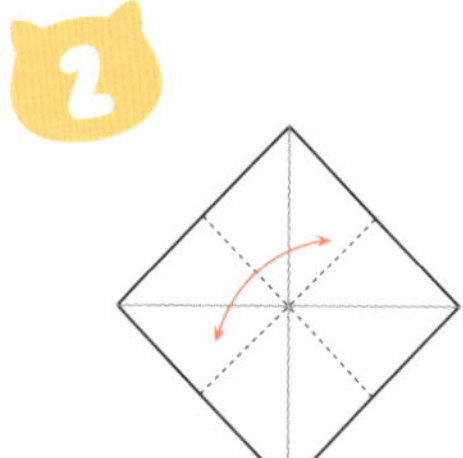

2

Now fold the other two diagonals and open the sheet again.

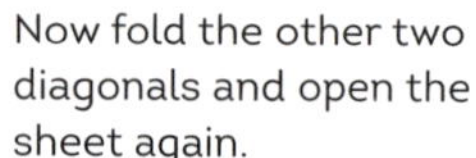

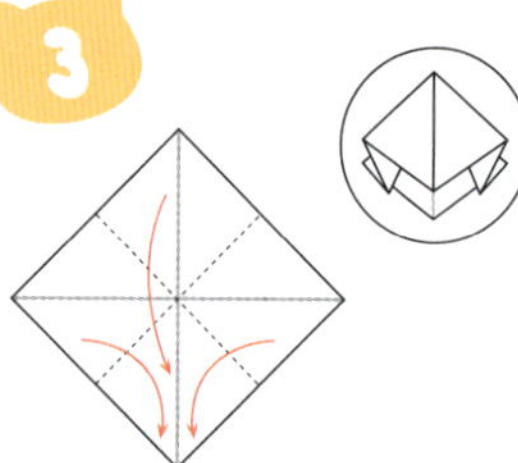

3

Place one finger on the center of the sheet so that the sides fold up. Now push the pre-folded shape together.

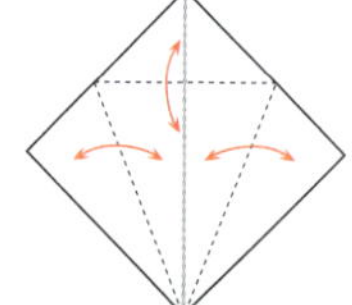

4

Place the folded piece in front of you with the open tip facing you. Fold the left and right edges to the center line and then fold the top tip down.

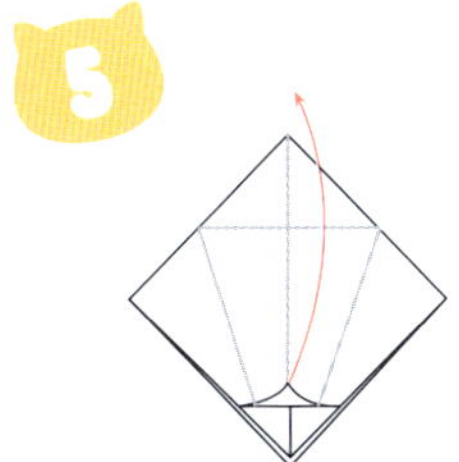

Fold the bottom corner upwards, automatically folding the outer edges toward the center.

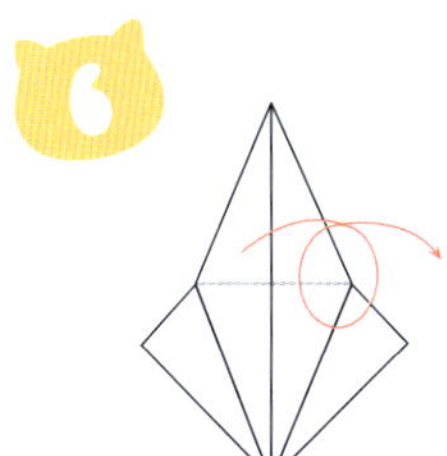

Turn the folded piece over and fold the bottom corner upwards as in the previous step.

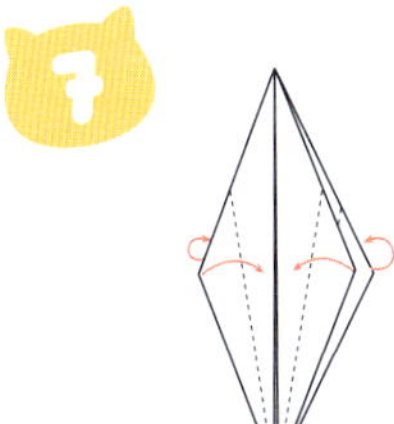

Fold the left and right corners toward the center. Turn the folded piece over and repeat the process on the other side.

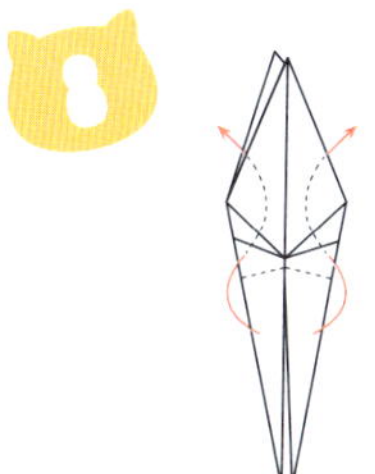

Fold the crane's tail and neck with two inner counterfolds.

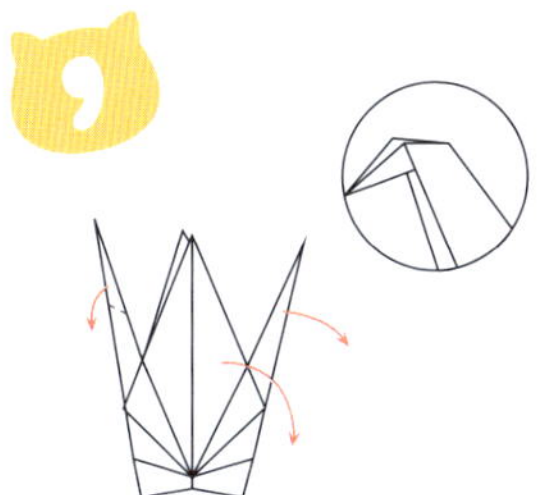

Now form the head with an inner counterfold and fold the wings to the sides.

Gift Box

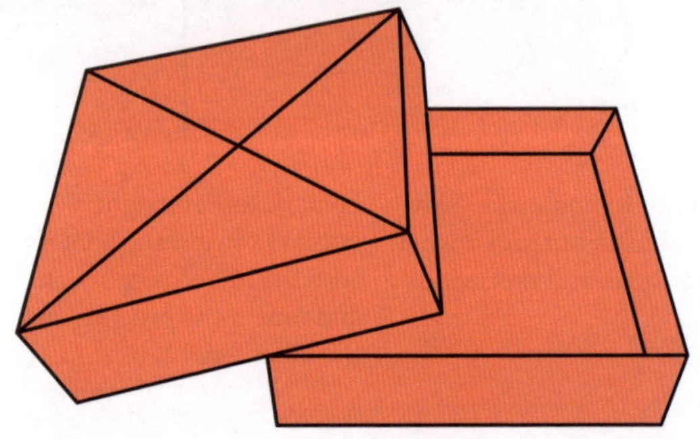

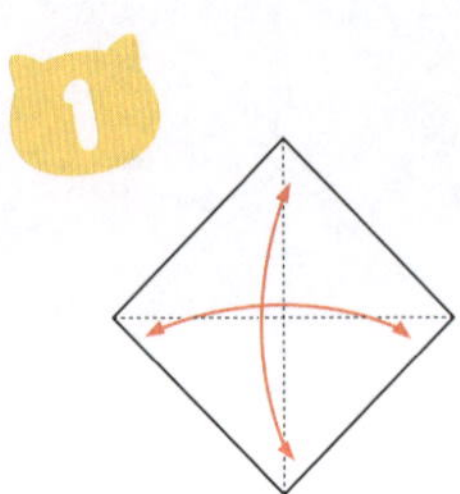

1

Fold the left corner over the right corner and back again. Then fold the bottom corner over the top corner and back again.

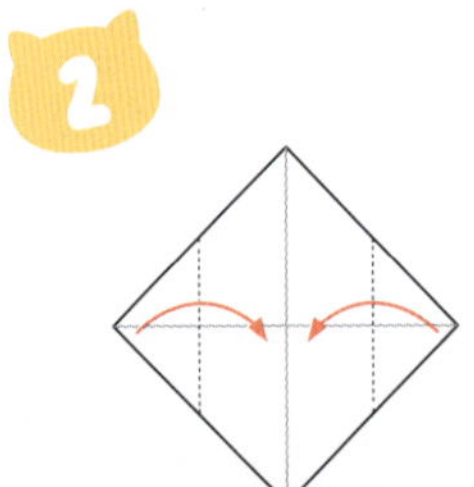

2

Fold the left and right corners to the center of the paper.

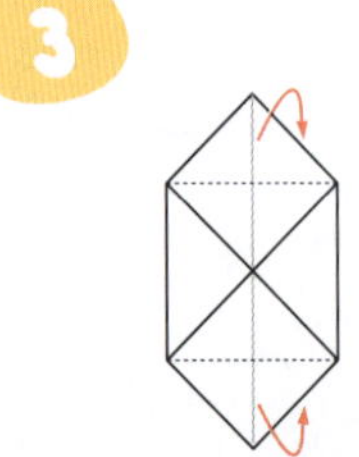

3

Now fold the top and bottom corners to the center—but towards the back!

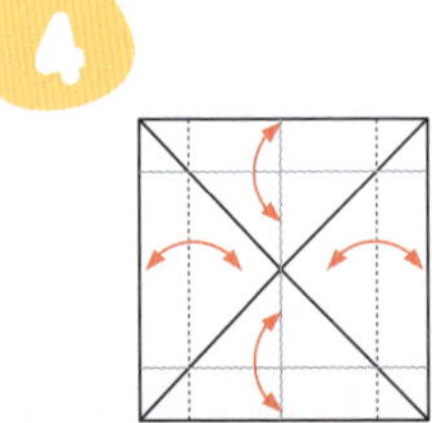

4

Fold the top edge down one-third of the way down and back again. Do the same with the bottom edge, the left and right outer edges.

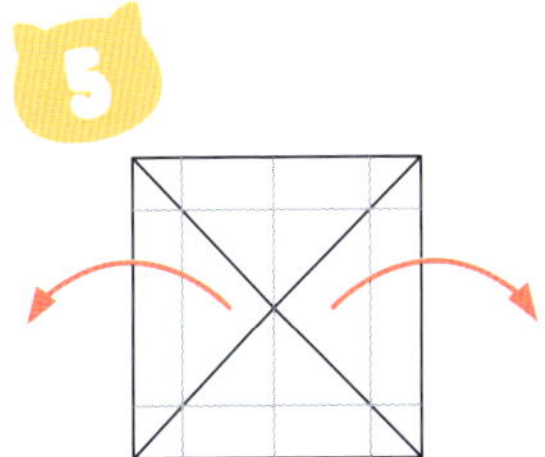

Fold the corners outwards again in the middle.

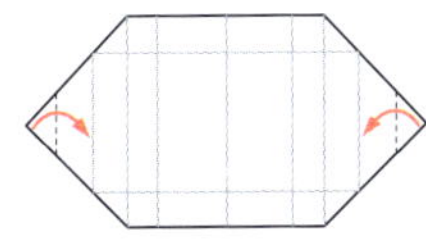

Now fold the left and right corners to the outermost fold line on each side.

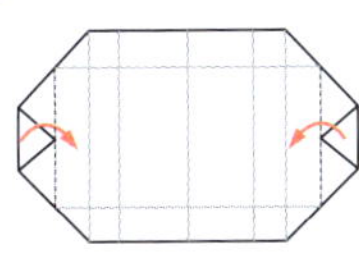

Fold the left and right outer edges again, each one to the next fold line toward the center.

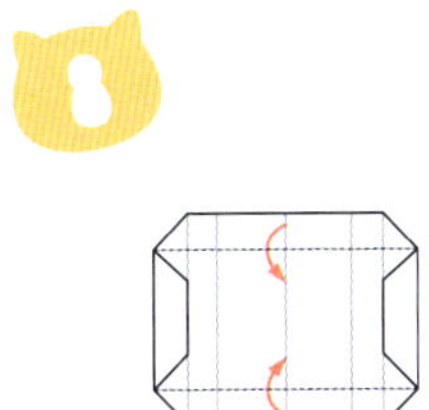

Fold the top and bottom edges along the existing fold line toward the center so that they point vertically upwards.

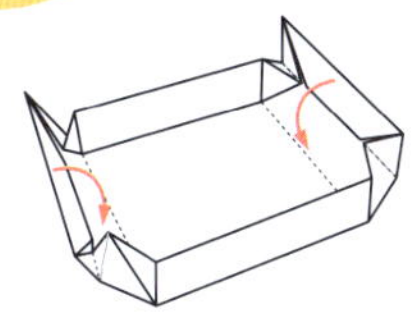

Fold the outer side edges vertically upwards along the third fold line from the outside. Fold the top half down over the side flaps.

To ensure the lid fits over the base, take a new piece of paper and cut off a $\frac{3}{16}$″-wide strip on each side. Repeat all steps.

Wreath of Stars

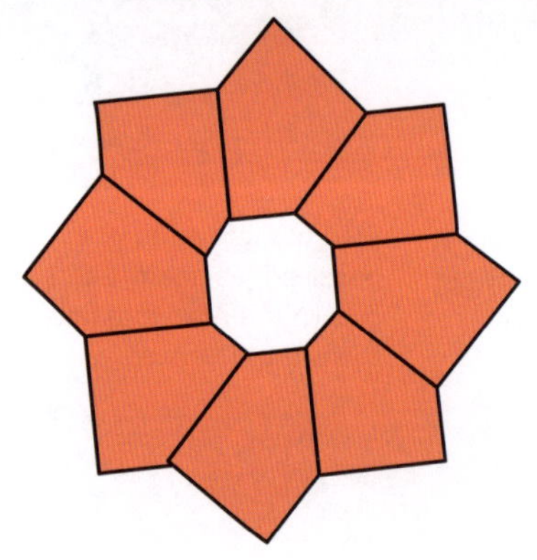

For this little star, you need to cut four square sheets in half. This will give you eight rectangles.

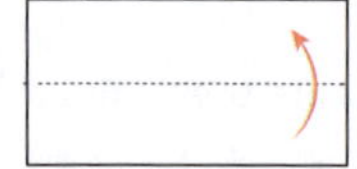

Then fold each rectangle upwards.

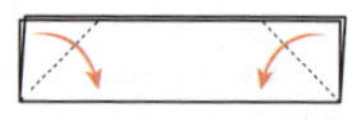

Fold the left and right corners down.

Now fold the rectangle to the right.

Repeat this with the other rectangles until all 8 pieces are finished.

Now, along the short, straight edge of the first wing, push the tip of the second wing between the two outer pockets.

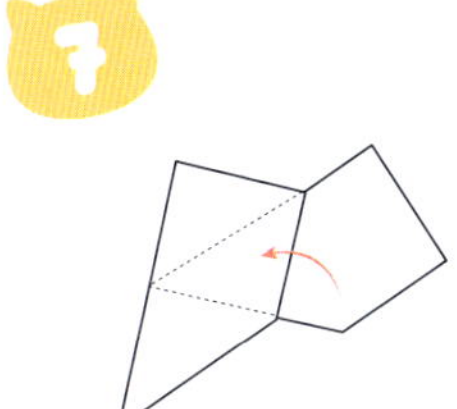

Push the second wing firmly in.

Once you have put all the pieces together, push the last point into the pockets of the first wing to complete your star wreath.

333 Origami Sheets Kawaii Kittens Designs

First published in the United States in 2025 by C&T Publishing, Inc., P.O. Box 1456, Lafayette, CA 94549

www.emf-verlag.de

This edition of "333 ORIGAMI – KAWAII KITTENS DESIGNS" first published in Germany by Edition Michael Fischer GmbH in 2024 is published by arrangement with Silke Bruenink Agency, Munich, Germany.

PUBLISHER: Amy Barrett-Daffin

CREATIVE DIRECTOR: Gailen Runge

SENIOR ACQUISITIONS EDITOR: Roxane Cerda

PRODUCT MANAGER: Betsy La Honta

ENGLISH-LANGUAGE COVER DESIGNER: April Mostek

ENGLISH TRANSLATION: Betsy La Honta and Gailen Runge

PRODUCTION COORDINATOR: Zinnia Heinzmann

Instructions: heart, fish, windmill, flower, crane: EMF; cat, butterfly, fox, rabbit, gift: Thade Precht; star wreath: Ina Mielkau; butterfly: © Hipatia/Shutterstock

Folding symbols: heart, fish, windmill, flower, and crane: © tofang/Shutterstock

Image credits:

Cover: © ma_nud_sen/Shutterstock, © NSTIvectors/Shutterstock, © ma_nud_sen/Shutterstock

Sample yellow: © Marina Zakharova/Shutterstock, © svtdesign/Shutterstock, © Aksenova Nadezhda/Shutterstock, © ma_nud_sen/Shutterstock, © Elmiral/Shutterstock, © Linda Ayu Pertiwi/Shutterstock, © NSTIvectors/Shutterstock

Pattern light blue: © Dma_nud_sen/Shutterstock, © psmxp/Shutterstock, © Eka Panova/Shutterstock, © Febi store/Shutterstock, © 4691/Shutterstock, © Mbukimbuki/Shutterstock, © LydiaLyd/Shutterstock, © NSTIvectors/Shutterstock

Pattern pink: © NSTIvectors/Shutterstock, © Sudowoodo/Shutterstock, © MKE design/Shutterstock, © Mbukimbuki/Shutterstock, © Aleandro/Shutterstock, © Linda Ayu Pertiwi/Shutterstock, © NSTIvectors/Shutterstock, © Inna Tan/Shutterstock

Pattern gray: © CraftCloud/Shutterstock, © molua/Shutterstock, © Mbukimbuki/Shutterstock, © NSTIvectors/Shutterstock, © Linda Ayu Pertiwi/Shutterstock, © JIMMOYHT/Shutterstock, © molua/Shutterstock, © svtdesign/Shutterstock

Pattern colorful: © ma_nud_sen/Shutterstock, © NSTIvectors/Shutterstock, © svtdesign/Shutterstock, © NSTIvectors/Shutterstock, © Linda Ayu Pertiwi/Shutterstock, © Linda Ayu Pertiwi/Shutterstock, © Lova Mikhailova/Shutterstock, © ma_nud_sen/Shutterstock

Printed in China

10 9 8 7 6 5 4 3 2 1

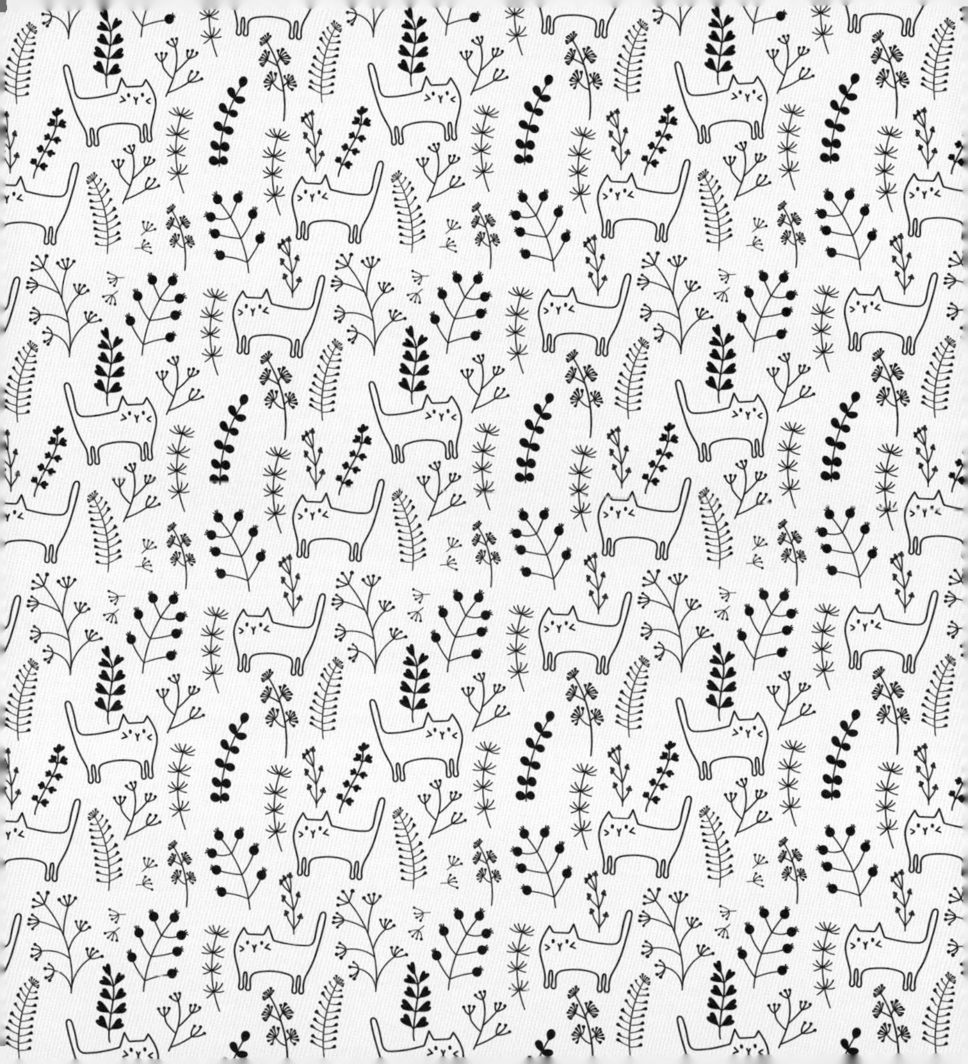

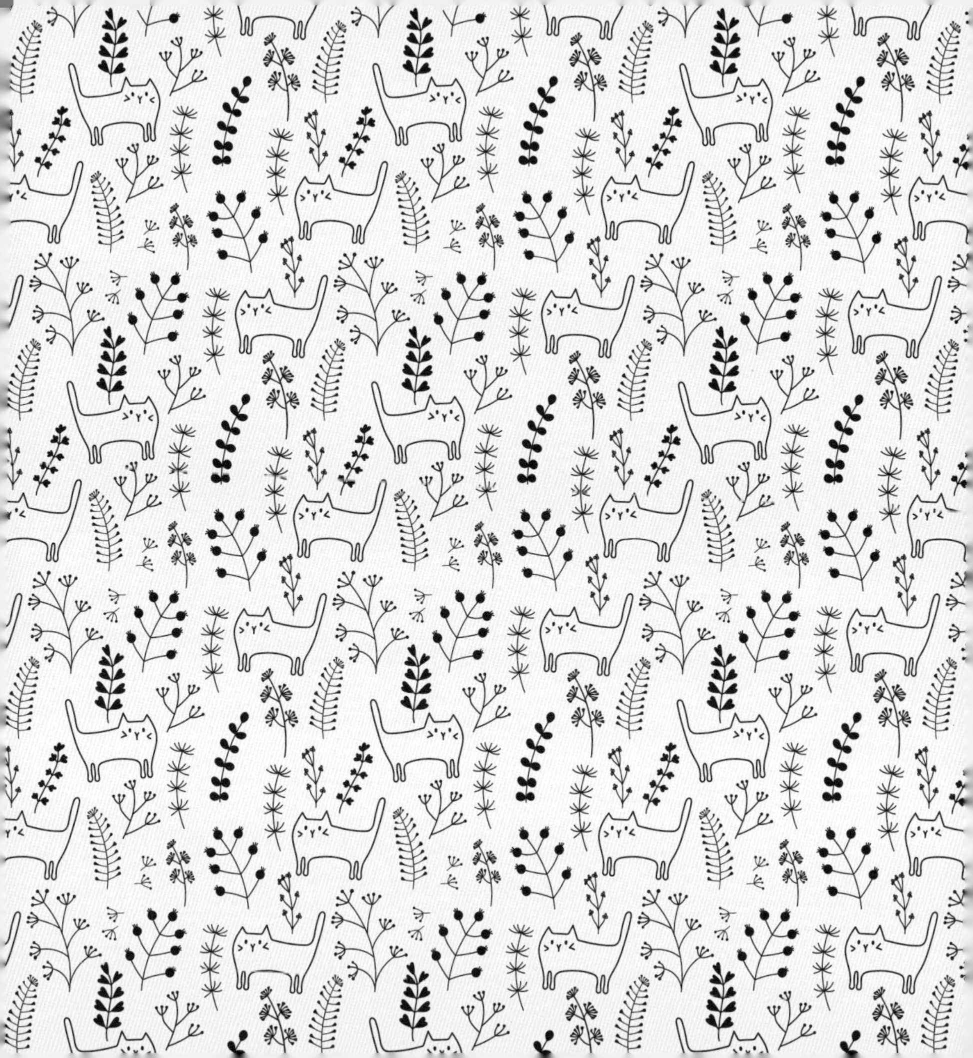

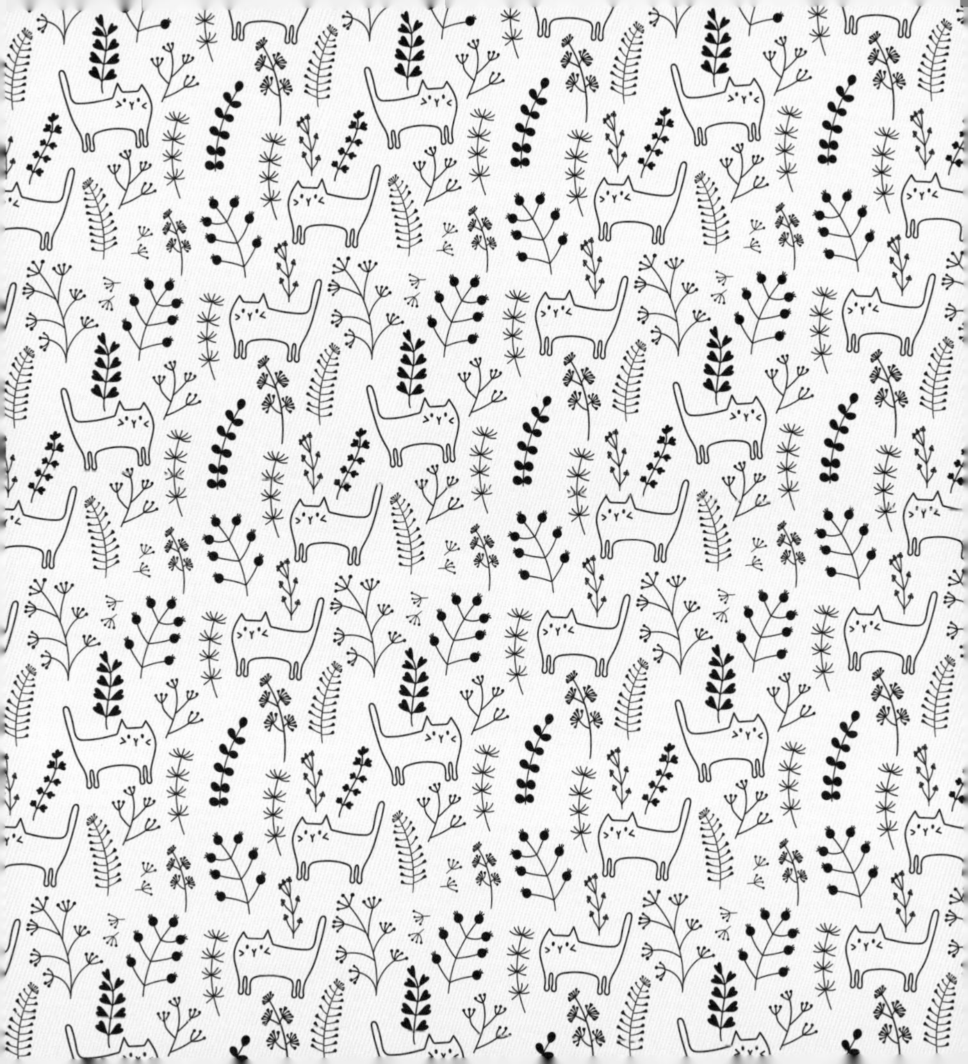

WH? AT.

WH?
AT

WH? AT.

WH? AT.

WH? AT.

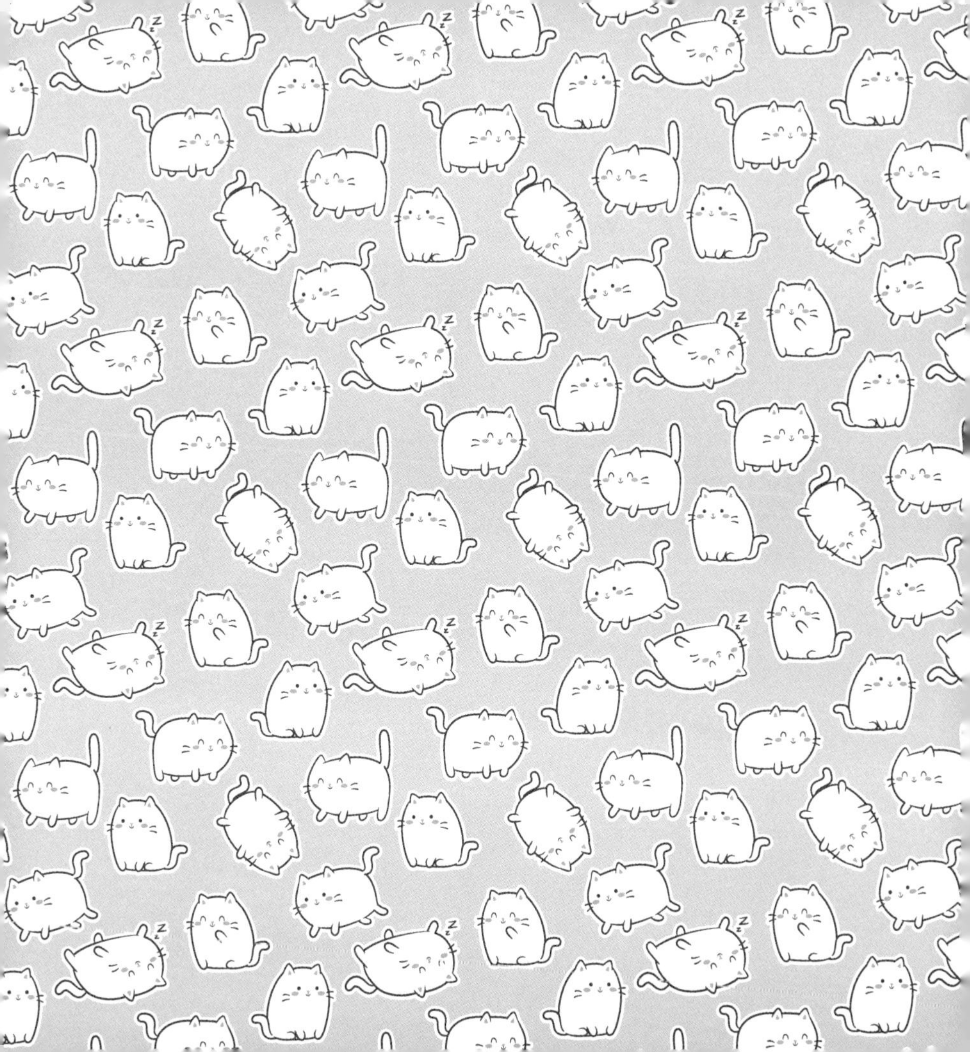

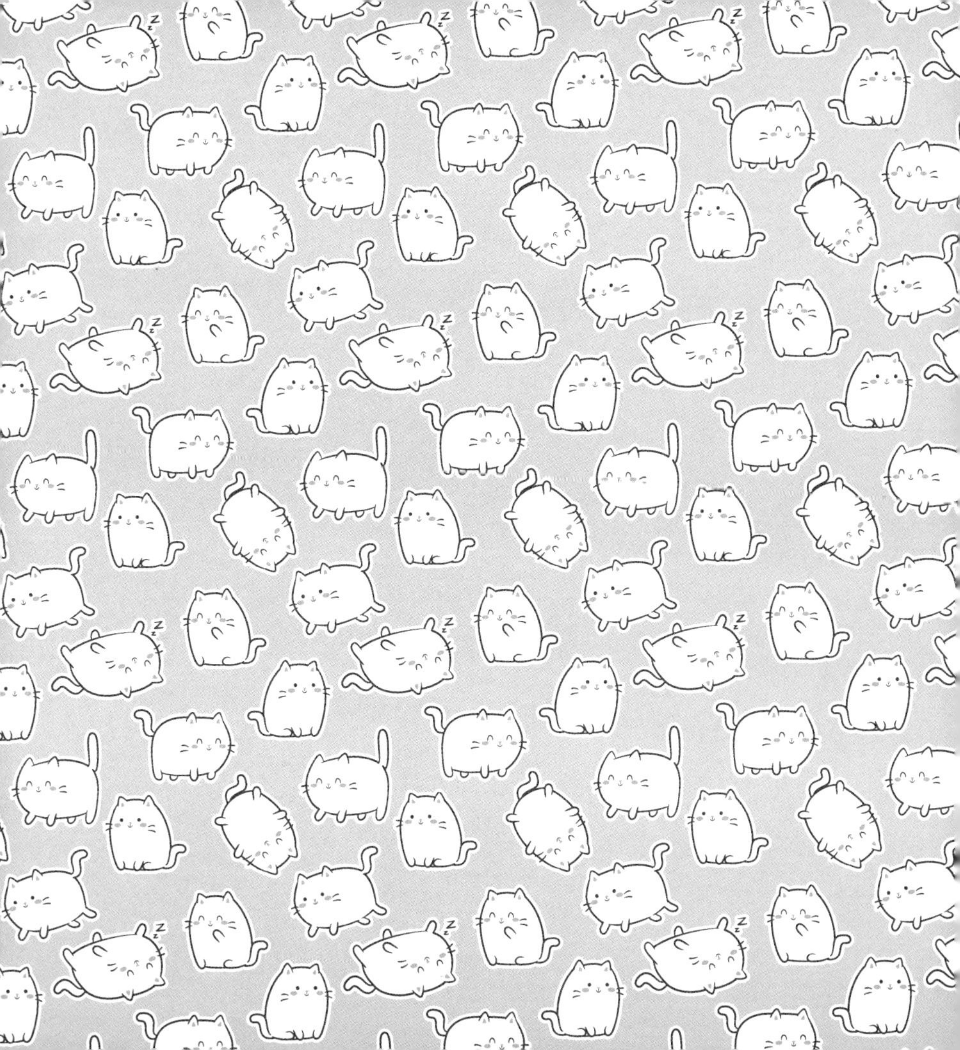